The Ultimate Collection of Unicorn Facts for Kids

Including 40+ Unicorn pictures

Ben Haydock

The unicorn is a mythical and legendary creature that exists in many legends and children's stories. They are often thought to be a pure white horse-like animal with a single horn protruding from the head, but that has not always been the case.

To this day, many believe that unicorns are real and once roamed the earth, whereas some think they exist only in mythical stories. There have been many hoaxes and claims of the discovery of unicorns throughout history including stories from many famous and well-respected individuals.

There are many mysteries surrounding the legend of unicorns, so here is the Ultimate Collection of Unicorn Facts for Kids.

The word *unicorn* literally translates to "one-horn". It comes from the Latin word *unus*, which means one, and *cornu* which means horn.

A picture of a unicorn with two horns was found in the Lascaux Caves in France dating back to 15,000 BCE.

Many believe that good luck will arrive upon seeing a unicorn.

The earliest mention of a unicorn in western literature appeared in the work of Ctesias from the 5th century BCE. The unicorn had a purple head with blue eyes, a white body, and a horn that was red, black, and white.

Genghis Khan believed he saw a unicorn while on his way to conquer India. Thinking it was a sign from his deceased father to turn back, he did.

Marco Polo believed he encountered unicorns on his travels when he had actually encountered Rhinoceroses. He described it as "a passing ugly beast to look upon, and is not in the least that which our stories tell of."

The horn of a unicorn is known as an alicorn.

Alicorn is also the name for a horse with wings and one horn.

Many famous people throughout history have claimed to see unicorns, even Julius Caesar once described a unicorn he had seen. He described them as an "ox-like stag" with a straight and long horn in the forehead.

The King James version of the Old Testament included nine references to unicorns. However, these were translation errors.

In the 1400s there were gold coins known as the unicorn and the half-unicorn.

Unicorn horns were once worth a lot of money. The pope even bought a unicorn horn from German merchants in 1560 for a significant sum of money.

Pharmacies in London, England sold powered unicorn horn until at least 1741.

Lake Superior State University in Michigan can issue unicorn hunting permits, which allow a hunter to carry pinking shears and a flask of cognac since 1971.

From the creation of unicorn hunting permits, a group dedicated to staking out and hunting unicorns was created. "The Unicorn Hunters" group disbanded again in 1987.

Narwhal tusks were sold as unicorn horns throughout the Middle Ages and the Renaissance.

There is a species of unicorn called the Pegasi, they are described to have large wings and the ability to fly. Pegasus is an example of a winged horse however, Pegasus is not a unicorn.

There is mystery surrounding the unicorn. European folklore describes unicorns to be wild and unable to be tamed, but other countries have depicted them as gentle and docile creatures.

Many movies, books, and TV shows have featured unicorns including Harry Potter, My Little Pony, and Buttercup in Toy Story 3.

Narwhals have a tusk that is thought to look like a unicorn horn which can grow up to 10 feet long.

Unicorn horns became a staple in early apothecaries due to claims that they could protect against poisons. Queen Elizabeth even owned a cup thought to be made from one.

The modern-day interest in unicorns came from the 1968 fantasy book "The Last Unicorn" where all but one unicorn are turned into narwhals.

One of the most valuable Beanie Babies in existence was Mystic the Unicorn, which was first released in 1994. One was listed for $3,750.

Texts dating back to the 14th century claimed that unicorns could purify water by touching it with their horn.

The unicorn appears in the art of ancient Mesopotamia which dates back to 5,000 BCE.

The unicorn is thought to hold the power to divine truth and will pierce the heart of a liar with its horn.

According to Jewish legend, the unicorn is strong enough to be able to easily kill an elephant due to its immense power.

The Scottish unicorn is found on the United Kingdom's Royal coat of arms and has a tail that resembles a lion.

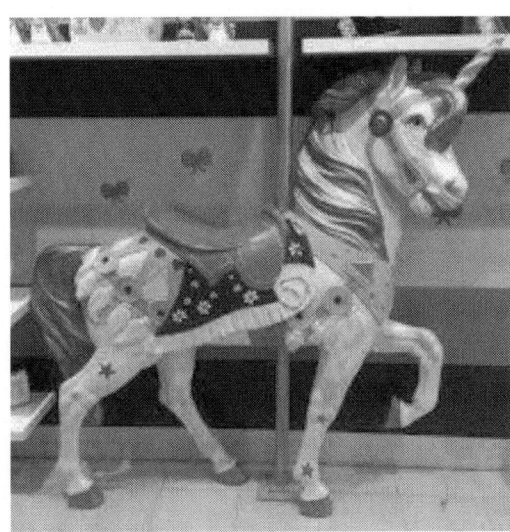

It is believed that the unicorn is attracted to purity and innocence. This has lead to the legend of the virgin and the unicorn, where a unicorn will lay down and place its head on the lap of someone beautiful and pure.

The unicorn is known to symbolize innocence, purity, and femininity. It is often seen as the counterpart of a lion, which is thought to symbolize masculinity.

Some pictures show unicorns to have the feet of a goat or the tail of a lion.

Old tapestries show unicorns to have wispy goat-like beards, but modern descriptions of unicorns depict unicorns to be pure white with long, tapering horns, cloven hooves, and graceful bodies.

Unicorns are thought to live in forests throughout places like Europe, Asia, and India.

Christian legends describe the Unicorn to be as small as a normal sized goat and so fearful that no hunter would be able to catch one.

Claudius Aelianus was a roman author, who claimed that India has a one-horned horse in his work "On the Nature of Animals."

It is believed that if the horn of a unicorn was to be placed on an injury, it would heal the wound.

In Medieval times, possession of even a fragment of a unicorn's horn was thought to be able to prolong the life of a person.

In 1577, Queen Elizabeth was presented with a narwhal tusk believed to be the horn of a unicorn. It was given a value of between 10,000 and 40,000 pounds. To this day it is still considered to be a royal treasure.

"Natural History" was a piece of encyclopedic work by Roman naturalist Pliny the Elder which included unicorns. This was understood to be factual for over 1,600 years.

Many believe that unicorns are like the dodo, and were alive at some point but were hunted to extinction.

In 1994, a beautiful and carved "unicorn horn" was auctioned in London for 500,000 pounds.

Due to the belief that they were able to protect against poison, it was a custom in France to carry a cup made from the horn of unicorn to test whether the food and drinks were poisoned until the late 18th century.

Unicorns occupy a significant place in Chinese mythology, where they are known as a Ki-Lin or Chi-Lin.

The ancient Chinese believed unicorns had a very long life, living up to 1000 years and were an embodiment of wisdom and knowledge.

Chi-Lin are thought to have a beautiful voice and be an extremely gentle animal.

The ancient Chinese believed a unicorn to be a harbinger of great fortune and good luck.

Chinese unicorns are described significantly differently to the European unicorn. Chi-Lin was a combination of a lion and a dragon, the single horn was short and it grew backward.

In Chinese legends, unicorns would appear at the time of birth of wise men and emperors.

According to Chinese mythology, a unicorn appeared at the time of birth of Confucius, a Chinese philosopher. The unicorn was carrying a piece of imperial jade in its mouth which contained the prophecy of the baby.

In the Bible, the Old Testament mentions that unicorns lived in the "Garden of Eden". They are even painted on biblical tapestries in Europe. Some theologians claim that unicorns then perished in the Great Flood.

The Vikings of Norway used to use the tooth of narwhal to trade during the 17th century, where it became quite valuable. It was thought the cure diseases and prove whether a noble maiden was a virgin.

Sir John Mandeville wrote a book about travelers tales in 1357. In this, he mentioned that unicorns are a real animal and this was considered reliable for many years.

Until the mid 17th century, missionaries and monks would often recount real sightings of unicorns.

Alexander the Great believed he had a few encounters with an animal with the head of a lion and the body of a horse. This animal was called Bucephalus and was thought to be a possible unicorn sighting.

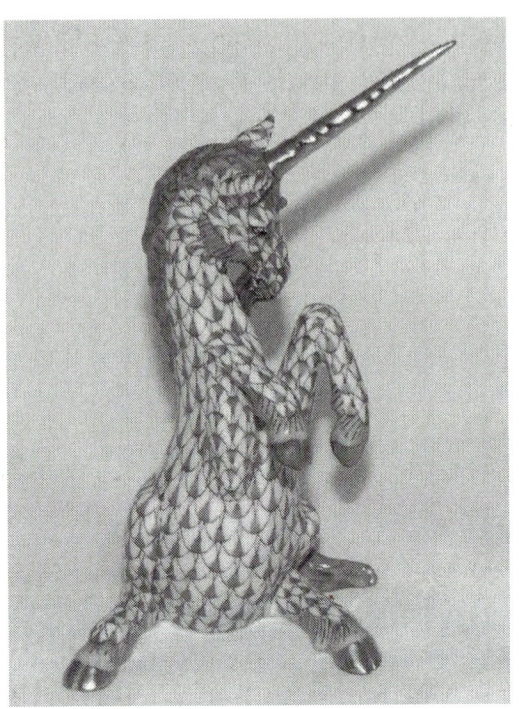

Seals have been found portraying an animal with a horn during the Indus Valley Civilization.

During the Dark Ages, there were collections known as bestiaries. These listed known animals with their biological properties and medicinal use, and included unicorns. This is where it was first determined that virgins had great power over the creatures.

At the height of its value, "unicorn horn" was sold for the equivalent of 10 times its weight in gold.

Unicorns can be found on the ancient seals of Babylonia and Assyria

The giant rhinoceros of Siberia which roamed the earth until 29,000 years ago is also known as the one-horned Siberian unicorn. However, they are now extinct and resemble a rhino rather than a unicorn.

The Siberian unicorn was six feet tall, 15 feet long, and weight around 9,000 pounds.

It is a common opinion that all unicorns are male.

In 1985, the Ringling Bros. circus had a unicorn as one of their attractions. What they were passing off as a unicorn was actually a goat, called Lancelot, whose horns had fused together.

Unicorns are the national animal of Scotland and appear on many coats of arms throughout Europe.

A US patent was granted in the 1980s for the creation of unicorns using a surgical procedure. This surgery included transplanting the horn buds of a goat, creating one horn in the middle of the head.

National Unicorn Day is celebrated on the 9th of April every year in Scotland.

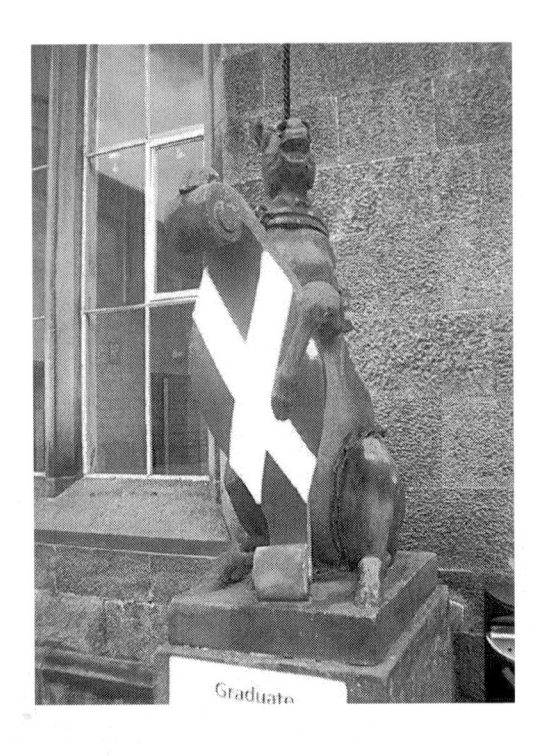

The United States has also started celebrating National Unicorn Day on the 9th of April since 2015.

The North Korean government's official news outlet claimed that scientists reconfirmed the location of the resting place of a unicorn ridden by the founder of the ancient Goguryeo kingdom in November 2012.

Saint Isidore, Archbishop of Seville insisted one could capture a unicorn by using a female virgin, which then became a common belief.

Saint Isidore also claimed unicorns to be strong and fierce, and known to fight and kill elephants.

In the late 1600s, the Throne of Denmark was constructed. The throne includes spiraling white spokes and legs that are thought to made from unicorn horn.

Unicorns were often portrayed in Christian art during the Renaissance, even being used as a metaphor for Christ. They were thought to represent love and chastity.

There is now a parody religion known as the Church of the Invisible Pink Unicorn, where a pink unicorn is used to symbolize skepticism of religion.

Although not actually unicorns, there have been several cases of deer being born with a single horn, including one in Italy in 2008 which was given unicorn as a nickname.

Self-proclaimed wizard Oberon Zell would breed one-horned goats after developing an obsession with unicorns from reading the novel "The Last Unicorn".

A rock band known as The Unicorns were formed in 2000. Unfortunately, after only releasing one album, they broke up in 2004.

Unicorns have become extremely popular in pop-culture, creating many unicorn themed items including unicorn toast, unicorn cupcakes, and unicorn hair.

Unicorns are thought to be quite vain and enamored of themselves. They have been described to spend hours admiring themselves in mirrors.

The Unicornfish gets the name from a horn-like appendage between the eyes, scientists are unsure what the horn is used for.

In Germany, there is Unicorn Cave where prehistoric bones were found and thought to be from unicorns. It was later discovered that the bones were actually from bones of mammoths and rhinos with the horn from a narwhal.

It is thought that travelers from Arabia mistook antelopes for unicorns due to seeing them from the side, where their two horns looked like one.

There is a reported unicorn horn in Scotland at the castle of the chief of the Clan MacLeod. It was later identified as the horn of an eland, an antelope from southern Africa.

The old Turkish reports of unicorns, called karkadann, or kartijan, describe them as a ferocious beast with a massive body and one horn. The karkadann was able to outrun all other beasts of the forest with thundering steps that would shake the earth. It would bellow to scare away all animals except for the ringdove, whose song was thought to lull the beast.

In Christianity, the unicorn became associated the Virgin Mary, which led to the symbolism of unicorns as pure and gentle creatures able to discern truth.

Some believe that unicorns took to the sea to avoid being hunted, where they adapted to become narwhals.

Many countries have developed their own unicorn-esque legends. In Japan, there is the kirin. The kirin is a fierce creature who was known to pierce the hearts of evil people with their horn.

Thanks for reading *The Ultimate Collection of Unicorn Facts for Kids.* You must be an expert by now, so you can show off everything you know to your friends!

If you have enjoyed this book, please leave a *review* on Amazon and check out our other publications.

Printed in Great Britain
by Amazon